Deserts

Steck Vaughn™

HOUGHTON MIFFLIN HARCOURT
Supplemental Publishers

www.SteckVaughn.com
800-531-5015

Deserts

contents

Deserts
Fact Matters

ISBN-13: 978-1-4190-5456-3
ISBN-10: 1-4190-5456-2

First published by Blake Education Pty Ltd as *Go Facts*
Copyright © 2006 Blake Publishing
This edition copyright under license from Blake Education Pty Ltd
© 2010 Steck-Vaughn, an imprint of HMH Supplemental Publishers Inc.

Printed in China

4 5 6 7 8   0940   15 14 13 12
4500367890

What Are Deserts?

Deserts are dry places. They get less than 10 inches of rain or snow each year.

There are two main types of deserts. There are hot deserts and cold deserts. Hot deserts have a lot of sand or rock. They have very high temperatures in summer. Hot deserts are usually at low **elevations**. The air is very dry. There are few clouds. The temperature can drop below freezing at night.

Cold deserts have sand, rocks, and ice. Cold deserts are at higher elevations. It is cooler at high elevations.

Antarctica is an example of a cold desert. It often snows in cold deserts.

The barrel cactus stores water.

Libya had the highest recorded temperature on Earth. It was 135 degrees Fahrenheit. Antarctica had the lowest temperature. It was minus 128 degrees Fahrenheit.

The Gobi Desert in Mongolia is a cold desert.

Antarctica is the driest continent on Earth.

Australian deserts are hot deserts.

Deserts of the World

Each desert is different. All deserts have common features.

The features of a desert depend on **erosion**. Erosion is the effect of wind and water on rock. It doesn't rain much in the desert. Sometimes there are rainstorms. This rain quickly erodes rocks. Wind erodes rocks slowly and **constantly**.

Soft rocks are eroded to **fine** grains of sand. Winds push the sand into dunes. Windstorms carry sand dunes over great distances.

Hard rocks are eroded to stones and pebbles. Nearly half of the world's deserts are plains. They are covered with rocks and pebbles. Only 20 percent of deserts are covered in sand.

The blue-tongued lizard lives in Australian deserts and forests.

Sand dunes can reach 1,300 feet high.

Kata Tjuta in Australia's Central Desert was formed by the erosion of mountains.

These rock formations in Monument Valley, Arizona were created by erosion.

Did You Know?

Sand dunes can sing! Some sand dunes make a low rumble. The sound is caused by sand sliding down the sides of dunes.

You can find some water in deserts.

Some deserts have rivers and **oases**.

The Nile and Colorado rivers run through deserts. The soil soaks up some water from the rivers. A lot of water **evaporates**. This is due to hot weather.

An oasis is a place with a reliable water supply. An oasis forms where underground water comes to the desert surface as a spring. People can make oases by digging wells.

Deserts of the World

1. Antarctic Desert
2. Arabian Desert
3. Atacama Desert
4. Chihuahuan Desert
5. Gibson Desert
6. Gobi Desert
7. Great Basin Desert
8. Great Sandy Desert
9. Great Victoria Desert
10. Dasht-e Kavir Desert
11. Kalahari Desert
12. Mojave Desert
13. Namib Desert
14. Sahara Desert
15. Sonoran Desert
16. Takla Makan Desert

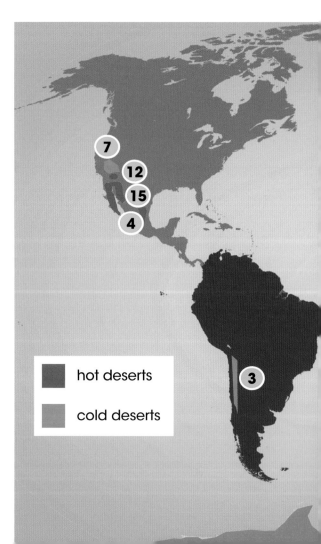

hot deserts

cold deserts

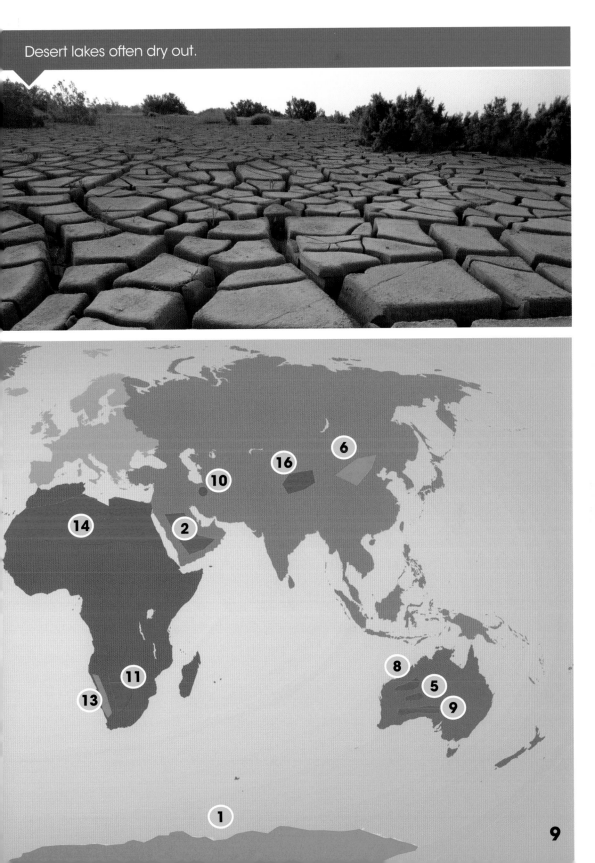

Desert lakes often dry out.

The Sahara

The Sahara is the largest hot desert on Earth. It covers one-third of Africa.

About one-quarter of the Sahara is made up of sand dunes and rocky **plateaus**. The rest of the desert is made up of gravel plains.

Plants, animals, and millions of people live in the Sahara. It can get hotter than 122 degrees Fahrenheit. The Sahara gets less than half an inch of rain each year. Sand and dust storms can blow for days. These storms make travel in the desert dangerous.

The Sahara has many oases. The oases are very far apart. People would not be able to live in the Sahara without oases.

Camels have been used to travel in deserts for thousands of years.

Some people who live in the Sahara are **nomads**. They have no fixed home. Instead, they travel from place to place.

People wear headdresses to protect their heads from cold and blowing sand.

Sahara comes from the Arabic word for desert.

Date palms grow at oases.

Desert Plants

Desert plants have special features. These features help the plants collect, store, and save water.

Some desert plants have roots that cover a wide area. These roots are just below the ground. Other plants have roots that go deep underground. Mosses and lichens get water from above the ground.

Many desert plants store water. They have hollow leaves, stems, or roots. These plants are called **succulents**. Succulents have thick skin and small leaves. They don't lose the water that they store.

Some desert plants only grow and flower after the rain falls. Some seeds lie on the ground for years. They start to grow when it rains. Dry grasses may look dead above ground. But their roots are still alive underground.

Aloe vera is a succulent. It is often used in cosmetics such as creams.

A saguaro cactus can grow 65 feet tall.

The spikes on a cactus keep animals from eating the plant.

The baobab tree stores water in its trunk.

The prickly pear cactus grows in deserts in the Southwest.

Did You Know?

The Sonora Desert in the United States and Mexico has more types of plants than any other desert in the world.

13

Desert Animals

*Desert animals conserve water. They try to **avoid** very hot and very cold temperatures.*

Animals get most of their water from the plants or animals they eat.

Reptiles store water and fat in their bodies. Gila monsters save fat in their large tails. More than 100 reptile species live in the Sahara.

The fur or hair of large desert animals keeps them cool. The outer layer of a camel's coat can be more than 80 degrees hotter than its body.

Some desert animals **burrow** underground to escape hot and cold temperatures. The marsupial mole is an example. The temperature is cooler underground in hot deserts. It is warmer underground in cold deserts.

Many hot desert animals are **nocturnal**. They sleep during the day. At night they move around. The addax is a nocturnal African antelope. It digs a hole with its hooves. Then it lies down in the hole during the hottest part of the day.

Geckos are nocturnal.

Penguins are desert animals.

Some desert birds cannot fly. This bird is a roadrunner.

The thorny devil drinks the dew that collects on its back.

Did You Know?

The largest scorpion in the world is the emperor scorpion. It is found in Western Africa. It can grow more than 7 inches long.

A Desert Food Chain

Some desert animals eat plants. Some desert animals eat other animals.

Many desert animals are both **predators** and **prey**. Survival depends on catching food but not being caught.

1 Plants make their own food from the energy of the sun.

2 Small animals and insects eat the seeds, leaves, and flowers of these plants.

3 Small predators eat the plant eaters and other small predators.

4 Large predators eat smaller predators and plant eaters.

Desert animals are often the same color as the ground. Predators can't see them.

1 prickly pear

2 jackrabbit

3 rattlesnake

4 golden eagle

Staying Cool

*Animals stay cool underground in a hot desert. The soil acts as an **insulator**.*

An insulator slows down or stops the movement of heat. Test how well soil works as an insulator.

What you need:

- two large tin cans
- two small tin cans
- two thermometers
- soil
- warm water
- a watch or clock
- pen and paper

Desert tortoises dig deep burrows. The burrows keep them cool during the day and warm at night.

1 Put warm water and a thermometer in each of the small cans.

2 Place each small can inside a large can.

3 Fill around ONE of the small cans with soil.

4 Write down the temperature of each of the thermometers. Repeat this step every 5 minutes for 30 minutes. What is happening to the temperatures?

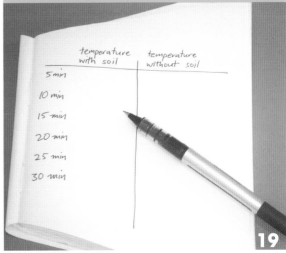

	temperature with soil	temperature without soil
5 min		
10 min		
15 min		
20 min		
25 min		
30 min		

Threats to Deserts

*Deserts are easily damaged. Mining and farms are the biggest **threat** to deserts.*

Deserts often contain oil and iron ore. Mining and drilling for oil can harm desert environments.

Tourists can damage desert water supplies. Vehicles can damage desert soil and plants.

Farms can damage the **fragile** desert soil. Farm animals pound the soil with their hooves. This breaks up the soil. The soil is then eroded by wind and rain. Farm animals also eat the plants that help hold the soil together.

Goats are raised in African deserts.

People hunted the oryx antelope until it was nearly **extinct**.

There are many oil wells and refineries in the deserts of the Middle East.

Some people treat deserts like trash dumps.

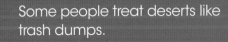

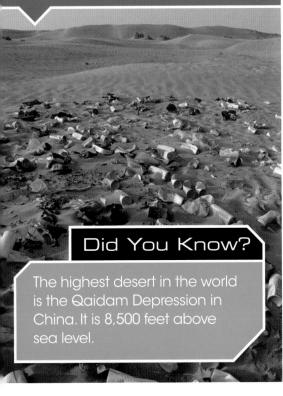

Did You Know?

The highest desert in the world is the Qaidam Depression in China. It is 8,500 feet above sea level.

Deserts are popular places to visit.

Desert Features

Rock		
Mesa	a large, isolated flat-topped rock	
Butte	a hill like a mesa, but with steeper sides	

Sand		
Erg	a large area of moving sand dunes	
Barchan	a sand dune with a curved ridge	

Glossary

avoid (uh VOYD) to keep away from

burrow (BUR oh) to dig a hole in the ground

constantly (KON stuhnt lee) always; without stopping

elevations (EHL uh VAY shuhns) heights above sea level

erosion (ih ROH zhuhn) the breaking down of rock by wind and water

extinct (ehk STIHNGKT) no longer alive or existing

evaporates (ih VAP uh rayts) changes from a liquid or solid to a gas

fine (fyn) very small or delicate; not coarse or heavy

fragile (FRAJ uhl) easily broken or damaged

insulator (IHN suh LAY tuhr) a material that electricity, heat, or sound cannot go through

nocturnal (nok TUR nuhl) active during the night

nomads (NOH mads) people who move around rather than live in one place

oases (oh AY seez) fertile spots in the desert where there is water

plateaus (pla TOHS) large, flat areas of land, high above sea level

predators (PREHD uh tuhrs) animals that hunt, kill and eat other animals

prey (pray) an animal that is hunted and killed by another animal; to hunt or kill for food

succulents (SUHK yuh luhnts) plants that have thick and juicy leaves or stems

threat (threht) a sign or source of possible harm

Index